lyrics

POEMS BY

michael paul austern cohen

© 2021 by Michael Paul Austern Cohen

All rights reserved.
Manufactured in the United States of America
Book design: Keli Pharaoh
Library of Congress Control Number: 2021918367
ISBN 978-1-7379325-0-5

CONTENTS

I

Pendants   15

Pushin Bricks   17

Fiat   19

Grateful Monkeys   21

Rattan Man   23

Rear View   25

Blue Prisms   27

Tunnels   29

Beautiful Noise   31

Packages   33

Sandpits   35

Baskets   37

Tuned Out   39

god in my Bottle   41

II

an Other People's Word   45

Cliff Houses   47

Boots   49

Counting Cobras   51

Petulant Pistols   53

Desiree's Screw   55

in the Dirt   57

Cigarello Sermon   59

Catching Nails   61

Pouring Spiders   63

Clowns   65

Chit-Chat   67

Turbulence   69

III

Tin Whiskey   73

Blacktop   75

Dead Flowers   77

Coconut Dream   79

Lost Between the Freeways   81

Glass People   83

Flooded Floorboards   85

Save-A-Lot   87

Hong Kong Knees   89

Sandstruck Big Wheel   91

Lemonade Masquerade   93

Alley Walking the Auroras   95

Sideways   97

The Kitchen   99

Unstrung Sandals   101

for Agony and Beauty,
who fence post
the emotional palette
smearing paint across
my Life's canvass.

lyrics

I

Pendants

the Eye of Rah found my Neck,
in the Courtyard of the Christian Kings,
and Joined Me.

the Fleur de Lille found my Neck,
in the ancient Maze of Red Suns,
and Joined Me.

and through Time
they choked my Naked Neck,
searing the Cold Nights,
seizing my Breaths.

until the Day broke
beyond an Atlantic Expanse,
yielding the Moon's Depth
to the Morning Star.

and I could Breathe,
and Begin
Again.

Pushin Bricks

the Cobblestones all Crowded,
looking for their Grades,
clothed in Winter's Crush,
wearing Icy Shades.

Jokers sold their Tricks
on top of Table Clicks,
piling Reasons on their
Rhymes to make up Time.

my Pillow caught the Corner
of the Cinder Block Pole,
so I gave it to the Loner's Soul,
took the Bus to the Park,
and dissolved into Dark,
pushin Bricks on their Heads,
in Shoes without Treads.

Fiat

Fearless Figurines pounded Hillsides
on Sidewalks without Beats,
marching Faceless up the Streets.

Sky-Stretched Slanted Houses
showed me the Welcome Door,
to Stolen Stairs still resting
on their Borrowed Floor.

Seduced by her Shadow,
Crowded by her Walls,
watching Neon Lizards
take their Falls.

I found the Zone
that read Toll-Free,
where You were parked for Me,
wearing Magical
Red Dressed Mahogany Wheels,
to take Us away
on Your Sunset Heels.

Grateful Monkeys

her Eastern Star
sketched Acrylic Skies,
drawing Canyon's on the
Morning's Eyes.

Rivers left their Jungle Beds,
passing by the Grateful Monkeys
smoking Buddha Heads.

and the Old Man sewed a Stare
only Silent Grins can bare,
because he had Beautiful Things
to Share.

Rattan Man

the Rattan Man
weaved the Sidewalks,
stealing Chestnuts for his Bag,
what a Drag.

skirting People Zoos,
he slipped into The Cafe
inviting him to Stay.

Sound Bites came from
Someones he didn't really Know,
at least in that Show.

the Sign said "Welcome Back"
so he sat in the Place
he'd never been,
waiting on a Friend.

Rear View

The Rear View
doesn't care,
so Leave it There,

man
just Leave it There.

Blue Prisms

the Cypress with the Secrets
scattered in the Wind
traded Peril for a Circus
ringed by Nowheres to Rescind.

the Angry Man danced,
chorused by his Sandmen
shouting Tunes that painted Fences
bright with Technicolored Sounds.

Folded Pockets found their
Partners through Six Swinging Doors,
leaking Layered Topics,
staining Simple Floors.

when the Sky turned to Blue Prisms
marking the Night,
making Everything There Is,
just about Alright.

Tunnels

her Sunshine sang my Song,
runnin down the Ride-Along,
Slick Pavements sparkling Black
without a Crack, On-Track.

we dodged Dead-Ends picking Locks,
leavin Time to its Grind,
moving us Way Past the Skylines.

even Lost, I saw you
in the Tunnel,
Boots on my Shuttle.

and Now my Mornings
walk me round the Stars,
because you Are.

Beautiful Noise

walking through Reluctance,
brought me to the Show,
where Shuffled Footsteps
painted Faces in the Snow.

my Corner kept me Seated,
searching for my Morning Fix,
when the Sound Knots
started tying up the Mix.

Silence ran out stealing
all the Eight-Track Voids,
rolling out Red Carpets
for the Beautiful Noise.

Packages

Lucid in my Sky,
Boxed Seconds became Shapes
wrapped up in their Why.

Postmarked to hide,
the Packages stamped Send
had me Inside.

Sandpits

Magenta Airs
on Crimson Winds
baked pointless Moods
on Amber Panes.

Visions stretching Patience
pulled Hopes
across Dry Plains.

Dunes spinning Truth Walls
roped Footsteps
into Hypnotic Reigns.

stepping Sideways
through the Sandpits
to miss the Spinning Grains.

Baskets

Shaking Circles
shared some Truths,
so the Basket made its Round.

her Angels
in the Warehouse,
She sat There to be Found.

but the Basket
begged for Payment,
and She had None Around.

so the Room
filled Her in,
nothin's Green,
down Here on the Ground.

Tuned Out

Tuned Out,
can't find my Frequency.

Turned Down
by Cut-Ribbon Currency.

Switched Off,
Haze in my Headlights.

Sideways,
Lost in the Midnights.

Not Home,
Mud in Tin Mirrors.

Froze Up,
Greasing Front Gears.

Warm Down,
wrapped in White Noise.

Run Over
by Society Toys.

No Room
for Anything More.

please Man,
show me The Door.

god in my Bottle

on Hope's Horizons
I relinquished My Mind,
was that Blind?

Sinning Glasses sat staked
against the Leathered Dirt,
untethered from the Hurt.

There, cutting off
Seduction's Throttle,
I saw God in my Bottle.

II

an Other People's Word

Honesty is an
Other People's Word,
the kind Someone
wishes that they'd Heard.

Cliff Houses

Messages shape Moods
into Moons,
orbiting Liquid Tunes.

Cliff Dancers turn their
Canyon Heels on Tacks,
in Metered Acts.

Blue Ledges leak Stillness
through their Roles,
into Tidepools tying Souls.

Boots

Sex rested on her Rail,
Steel Tips drawing Curves,
hooking Gem-Belted Blue Jeans
heeled in Polished Verbs.

Rimbaud Flashes
fainted Careless Musings
coined to pay Lust's Toll,
surrendering Suede Nickels
for Coal.

Curving Windows fed their
Captive Fame,
while her Liquor-Bottled Boots
whispered my Name.

Counting Cobras

Venom Colors
gathered in their Box,
Moving Poisons
walled by Locks.

Rainbow Vipers
scaled their Rhymes,
relenting Lessons
on Sordid Vines.

Dreams
without volition ascend
Crayon Mazes,
quickening Dead-Ends.

unbroken Charities
counted up my Cobras,
and collected them at Last.

Petulant Pistols

Petulant Pistols
pounded Prayers
listless in their Nowheres,
watching Blind Nomads
scratch their Nothings,
pushing Checkered Curtains
past Hung Visions,
rusted from Drying Rains,
tangling the winless
Solid Lines.

Desiree's Screw

Desiree's Disguise
in Tiger Eyes
stitched my Senses to
the Rivets on her Jeans.

Standing Sideways
Crossing Breaths,
she Seared me to her
High-Heeled Soul.

Vanity Veiled Veneers
missed her Diamond-cut Kiss,
just like This.

then her Chain
called my Beat,
while her Wrench
turned my Screw.

in the Dirt

the Turnstile smiled,
waving me Through,
imagining Things To Do.

the Gate with Pens
and Forms spelled Fate,
but I saw No Place to Wait.

People There were Running
a Race I wasn't in,
but my Hand-Stamp said Win.

so I hosed away the Hurt,
and left the Mess,
Standing In the Dirt.

Cigarello Sermon

Crumbling Beige Tastes
caressed my Cornered Scarlet Stops,
hinting at my Future's Folding Hilltops.

West Winds weaved their Will
past the Green-Carpet Cafe Squares,
marking Mirrored Moments.

Savory Lights paved the
Hanging City's heights,
leaving me Black-tied,
preaching to Nearing Nights.

Catching Nails

the Nervous Stairs sat,
waiting out their Fate,
while Pale Windows
wearing Crosses
cast their Memories
on Painted Light,
under Cloudbreaks
dropping Skylights,
dodging Diamonds,
catching Nails.

Pouring Spiders

Preaching Palm Trees
pass Monkeys,
fastening Gold Rings
to watchful Magenta Kings.

Makeshift Moods seed
Jasmine Whites,
laddering Pinpoints
breaking Change
into Diamonds.

Print stained Stencils
hanging Ice,
harbor Her Muse,
while I wake to Sit,
pouring Spiders
from my Shoes.

Clowns

Masks painting
Foreign Lands
mix Glitter into Glazes
dreaming Faraway Fates,
for Rainy Day Dates.

Gone and Drawn,
just another Pawn
in the Waking's Lazy Dawn.

Chit-Chat

shut Down, sent Outside,
long way Around
the Downtown Ride.

never mind the Gold,
spell's been Broken
along Soul Road.

chit-chat go Away,
been too long to
play that Sway.

Turbulence

Spray-painted Clouds
poison Shadows
walking their Workweeks
in Uniforms
frozen with Chimes.

Checkers push Passion
across tales of
torn Red-Rag Roses
onto mixed
Meshed Cotton Minds.

and the Gilded Gatherings
mournfully toss
French Roasted Rhymes.

Tin Whiskey

Vinyl-visioned Captions
fold their Tinted Fears
into Hopes yet to Lose,

stacking Salted Letters
sorting Sadness,
locked inside
Bourbon-Blackened Whiskey Tins.

Blacktop

my Contest with
the Rainbow Sours
tuned me Tight,
so I took their Wheels
across the Blacktop,
dodging Orange Tangs
in Jumpsuits,
guarding Chapels,
ransoming their Breaths,
in Wonder for Life's
What's Nexts.

Dead Flowers

can't Feel the Ground,
no Freedom to care,
her Hair felt Sad.

no Goodbye again,
just a Slip out to
Smoke the Morning's Myths.

Flying Cold
I just can't Arrive,

watching White Vanagons
turn back the Hours,
bringing me Home to more
Dead Flowers.

Coconut Dream

in a Coconut Dream
she Screamed my name
on a Gameboard
going Backwards.

the Checkered Colors
didn't Add-Up
on the Dice,
so I rolled again,
but you don't get to go
Twice.

Back on Track
was Breaking my Back,
but I couldn't Shortcut
through the Sunshine.

so I spent My Time
steering Hurricanes
down Bowling Lanes
lined with Angels.

Lost Between the Freeways

Exotic Plazas
shedding Scents
stirred up their
Simple Airs
to the usual Nowheres,
letting Lateness
slide down the
Moving Lights,
tracing Songs
through Twisted Sidewalks,
trapped between
the Freeways.

Glass People

watching the Glass People
pass through their
Color-Crypted Moods,
staging Acts over
Polka-Dotted Steps,
dashing down Temperamental,
Fashion-Fused Promenades,
I felt Playful.

Flooded Floorboards

Stubborn Staircases
watched the High Tide
Flood the Floorboards
under my Weighted Steps.

then I saw his
Outstretched Hand,
and he was me,
disguised by Spotted Eyes,
sputtering Useless Lies,
waxing Wise.

Save-A-Lot

Down the Aisles
the Devils Smiled,
but I missed that Heat
and found my Seat,
swiveling to watch my
Direction turn toward
Transition.

the Detour seemed Okay,
but we never made it That Way,
ditching me
wandering the Asphalt,
wondering how I lost My Self
between the Lines
at a vacant Save-A-Lot.

Hong Kong Knees

Too Cool for School
VIP Hallway Chairs
gazed toward their Escapes,
exhaling the
Second Floor People
beyond Jade Drapes.

the Eager Masked Men
who pushed Steel Murals
across Winged Terrains
seemed so Sane,
so Mundane,
so Silver Rain,

drizzling down
Red and White
Safety Drains.

but all I could see
were the He's and She's
and Killer Bees,
knocking around in their
Hong Kong Knees.

Sandstruck Big Wheel

between Sky Rides
selling Services,
I sequenced Days into
Neon Chalk Calendars,
mapping Reminders
to blow back
Paralyzed Misperceptions
blocking the
World's Streets,
stuck watching
the Sun move,
riding a
Sandstruck Big Wheel
spincasting
Cellophane.

Lemonade Masquerade

her Golden Eyes stirred
Crumbled Starlashes into
Soul-Sugarcubed Cocktails,
pouring Lemonade Masquerades
on her Pinks from the Past,
stacked in Bookshelves
breathing her Whispers
through Pre-printed Poems.

Alley Walking the Auroras

I'm right Where I'm supposed to Be,
but there's Nothin Much to See,
and nothin's in the Orbit
that's always Buzzin me,
so instead of Pushing On,
I left that Sketch Undrawn,
and turned to Careless Tirades
spitting Yard Waste on the Lawn.

Down the Road a bit,
to Lift Off all the Fits,
I followed Yellow Shadows
shaken from their Tales,
leaving me Again, with
Frayed Ends to Mend,
Alley Walking through the Auroras.

Sideways

the metal Lead-Heads
soaking their Dust Parade
by the Blind Sky Rye
didn't need My Help
to get so High,
and for Once my feeling
Sideways didn't seem so
Side-by-Side.

The Kitchen

I wanted to Talk,
so I Cabbed with a Man
to a Hamburger Stand,
but No One there could Listen.

Still I felt kind of
Awake by Mistake,
so I Stuck Out the Morning
to see What it All might Bring.

Unstrung Sandals

my Heart U-Turned
to give Five Bucks
to the Frog playing Clarinets
next to Oranges
without Hands,
when a Starlit
bumped me Backwards,
clashing Comets across
Our Moment's Sands.

Circling me down
with her Tiger Frown,
she performed
Her Tricks,
just for Kicks,
wearing Eternally
Unstrung Sandals.

ACKNOWLEDGEMENTS

With eternal gratitude to
Shelley Barlas Nagel,
my therapist,
who helped me find appreciation
for my own expression,
and the courage to share it,
and to Keli Pharaoh,
my agent, editor and publisher,
for making this book possible
in all ways,
and for the warm hearth
she lends her artists.

Born in 1965, Michael is from the Monterey Peninsula.
He is an accomplished artist and poet. The paintings
featured are Michael's originals, and his artwork can
be found at gallery-mpac.com. He paints in Carmel,
California and Cape Hatteras, North Carolina, and writes
poetry throughout the world.